SMARTYpants
secrets

Overcoming
PROCRASTINATION

Putting Off Doing Those Things You Just Don't Want To Do...

D.R. Martin, PhD*
(*Personal human Development)

SmartyPants Press
Falmouth, Maine 04105
www.SmartyPantsSecrets.com

ISBN 13: 978-1-943971-06-0
ISBN 10: 1943971064

The SmartyPants Secrets Concept

A **SmartyPants Secret** is that **one piece of information** that you need to know to make every job a little bit, or maybe a lot, **easier**. Almost everything we do in life has a SmartyPants secret that to it, that knowing the "secret" would help tremendously in shortening the learning curve.

After experiencing many "a ha!" moments that were previous head bangers, I realized that there was a lot of grief – i.e. aggravation, wasted time, spent resources - that could have been saved if I had known to tap into the insider information that others had and I was lacking. A SmartyPants secret is that crucial bit of timely knowledge.

We all want a magic bullet answer that solves all of our problems in one fell swoop and makes everything go perfectly well, preferably in record time! We want that magic to happen right NOW, to be easily done, and to be preferably cheap, or at least not at great expense. There are a lot of demands on our unattainable magic ☺

For example, one day I looked at my face and damn if I didn't see a "sun spot" (nastily also called a "liver" spot) marring the surface of my otherwise smooth face on the right lower cheek. I scheduled an appointment at the dermatologist to verify the find and see if it could be lasered off. She sent me to an aesthetician who gave me some key information that made a huge difference in my decision of what to do next.

I was told that my even slightly darker (Asian) skin carries more pigment than Caucasian skin obviously. But what's not obvious is the way the body works, specifically the way the skin works, which is that when you wound the skin's surface, which laser surgery would certainly do, extra pigments rush to the spot to heal it (the "job" of pigment is to protect the underlying cells). The net result is that non-Caucasian skin heals into darker scabs and scars. (I have noticed this phenomena before but never made a direct connection.) Why then would I ever choose to have laser surgery on my face to remove a mark only to end up with an even darker mark? Yikes!

Obviously I wouldn't, but without this specialized knowledge about different results with different skin types, that even the dermatologist didn't know (yes, she was the recommender of the laser surgery option) I would've made a poor decision, with permanent negative results. A SmartyPants timely secret to the rescue!

Experts, who have hours of experience doing what the newbie is attempting to do, have expert knowledge, which may not be so secret, but it is **key information** that the novice greatly needs.

If you've ever struggled with something then learned the 'something' afterwards that caused you to say to yourself or to say aloud, "*Well, **if I only known THAT before I did this**, it would've made a world of difference!*" then you just learned a SmartyPants secret - the hard way.

The short SmartyPants Secrets books give you the secret that you need on a given topic, the most important piece of information that makes the greatest difference between easier success and hard-fought failure.

When I was young there was a professor at Cornell University, which in his obituary listed him as "***the last man to know everything.***" I was taken by the concept of anyone knowing everything there is to know contained in one brain. Oh, to have such a mind!

But **to know everything**, logical facts and figures, and **to be able to do everything** are **two different things**. Brain power doesn't equal skill and expertise.

Today that one brain that knows everything is the Internet. There is so much information today available on the Internet; we can all be like that professor at Cornell and have access to all knowledge at the click of our fingertips.

More knowledge than we could ever consume - **who has time** to go through it all? Most of the time **what you really want is to know is the crux of the subject** on hand, not the whole litany of everything imaginable that is available to know.

Tell me just what I need to know! (and I likely don't know what specific knowledge to ask for). It's literally impossible to know what you don't know. Let the expertise of knowledgeable others guide you.

If you are new to a topic the **SmartyPants secret can save you time and effort**, which are important to your success. Not a complete course on the topic, which you can certainly get elsewhere, the SmartyPants secrets concept is primarily to help you **not miss the key information needed for success**.

The building block of knowledge that the foundation rests upon; the Keystone or cornerstone knowledge makes a critical difference, especially when that knowledge that you do have, or think you have, is **faulty, incomplete or missing** entirely.

The concept of **social proof** states that when we have no prior experience in a given situation we rely on **others to show us the way**. We believe that lacking personal knowledge, that their situation is similar to our situation, and therefore what worked for them has a high probability of working for us.

We quiz others about our shared circumstances around the situation to verify that their solution is a good one. Plus, we think: *there's nothing to lose in trying since I don't have a better answer*.

Then when what worked for another doesn't happen to work for us, we are reminded that **we are all different people**, with different variables that impact success or failure. Some solutions to problems are hit or miss depending on who we are. And sometimes success depends on having and following the right key knowledge.

Solving problems is not the complete SmartyPants concept, although SmartyPants secrets can indeed offer real help for real problems. Rather the full concept is that having that key knowledge piece makes efforts easier and successful quicker; hopefully **avoiding having the problem in the first place**. We do anything in life because we have a goal to achieve. Reaching that goal successfully, quickly and easier than without knowing the SmartPants secret is the SmartyPants concept.

And because **all SmartyPants secrets have a physiological root**, grounded in our shared human biology, every SmartyPants secret is valid for everyone, no matter who you are. While we are all uniquely different from each other, we have a **common biology** consisting of inherited traits that stretch back to the Neanderthal era.

Applying a SmartyPants secret **will work for you no matter who you are**. And in our busy world, who doesn't want to save time and know the SmartyPants secret to anything?

Why ever risk hindering easier success by not knowing the core success secret?

PROCRASTINATION

Putting Off Doing Those Things You Just Don't Want To Do...

20% of Adults Self-Report as CHRONIC Procrastinators

Are you like 20% of Americans who self-report being a chronic procrastinator? Maybe your procrastination habit is simply annoying to you, OR maybe it's really hurting aspects of your life and you'd really like to get on top of changing this bad behavior.

20%

Procrastination Predicts Long-Term Problems

There are many reasons why we procrastinate, which can be problematic as procrastination can predict several long-term future problems, like **putting off saving for retirement**

Retirement just seems sooooo very far away... and there are more pressing things today to spend money on!

"I'll think about saving for my golden years later"

.... or putting off seeing the doctor for preventative health issues.

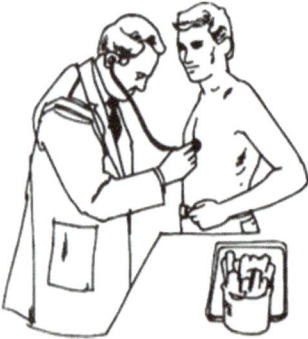

Ohhh, I don't like going to the doctor - you never know what he might find...

MEN Are Worse Procrastinators than Women for All Issues

Up to 70% of College Students Surveyed Are Procrastinators

- College students, especially males, heavily procrastinate
- Procrastinators tend to complete fewer years of education (for obvious reasons)
- Have a higher likelihood of unemployment
- Report lower salaries

Ouch! The tuition costs of procrastination are painful!!

So Why Is It That We Procrastinate?

Much of the time procrastination is simply a matter of **a lack of clarity** – we really don't know what's fully involved with completing a task, so lacking direction, **the task is a big scary unknown.**

At other times clarity isn't the problem but **negative thoughts** are, which invade our psyches and hinder our actions; negative thinking is really **self-doubt about what it is that you are about to undertake**.

Negative self-talk says things like:

> *"Why can't I ever seem to do what I know I should be doing?"*

> Or *"I know I should be more responsible and not put this off..."*

We beat ourselves up with these thoughts even as we continue to procrastinate taking the desired action.

At the Core of Procrastination is EMOTION

Emotion's little voice sounds in our head with, *"I'm a little uncomfortable right now so I don't feel like doing it... I'll feel so much better doing something that I want to do, which isn't this."*

Unfortunately procrastinating only causes the discomfort to get worse; when we procrastinate doing something for the short-lived good feeling that procrastination gives, we end up feeling worse afterwards, even more uncomfortable then when we first thought about procrastinating, so the negative feeling is compounded as worse than when we started.

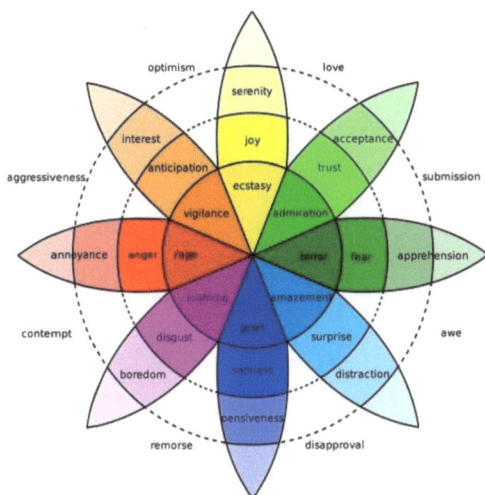

Procrastination Shares Some of the Same Features as ADDICTION

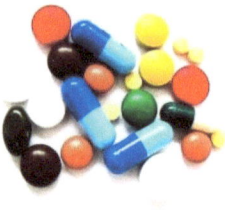

✓ Temporary feeling of excitement and pleasure -
Relieving the discomfort by giving into, "I don't want to do this and I'm not going to do it right now" gives a feeling of temporary pleasure and control.

✓ Relief from sometimes boring reality

The Thief of Time

Procrastination is the thief of time - a **hesitation caused by distraction, and inattention**.

 "It would be nice to take a few moments right now and surf the Internet" and with these words we convince ourselves that doing that exact activity is the best use of our time at any given moment. When procrastinating, we start to **tell stories to ourselves**.

We devise **creative but irrational excuses** that superficially make good sense:

"If I do this now something may change that could waste all my hard work, so I'm not going to start this too soon

because, who knows something might happen, and I don't want to have done all that work for nothing"

Silly excuses that seemingly make logical sense are just a way to procrastinate. We're good at talking ourselves into procrastinating by making up stories that we believe because they sound so reasonable in our head at the time.

In reality **procrastination can consume huge amounts of time and energy**. Procrastinating is a big **stressor** especially if you're a chronic procrastinator.

Procrastination Results in a Double Loss Time!

When we procrastinate something, we think we have put it aside, but it **lurks on the mental fringes of our thoughts**, not ever completely gone.

We continue to think about the activity that we have put off doing, even while we're doing something more enjoyable.

Our mind is still locked in on the item being procrastinated, **which ruins the enjoyment of the current pleasurable activity** – a double loss of time.

The Big Areas of Procrastination

Besides the little things, like procrastinating buying something that would be useful, let's focus on the bigger issues that are procrastinated:

At home – all those routine chores! (They're not called 'chores' for nothing!)

- ✓ balancing the checking account,
- ✓ doing taxes
- ✓ doing laundry
- ✓ doing the dishes
- ✓ paying the bills
- ✓ outdoor maintenance
- ✓ cleaning (windows, toilets, floors)
- ✓ etc, etc, etc

Distasteful tasks are easy to procrastinate!

With Relationships - obligatory social issues, which you would rather not, but feel that you must attend

- o undesirable family obligations
- o certain scheduled activities
- o certain people who are required company but not to our liking

The social occasions that have to be undertaken are procrastination targets

"Do we have *to go to your mother's house again this weekend?"*

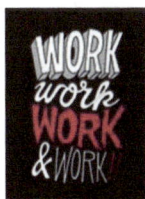

At work/school - perceived drudgery work is a big area of procrastination

"Yeah, I'll start that Big Project later when I feel more up to tackling it"

In **Health and well-being** activities – putting off doing those things (i.e. exercise) that we know we should be doing for long-term health benefits

"Gotta get to the gym today, but no time!"

Procrastination Isn't Always Bad – Is it a warning sign?

Procrastination *in moderation* can be a good thing; the motivating fear that procrastination can create **boosts adrenaline,** which gives more energy to complete the task, increases focus, and can cause us to work faster.

It's chronic procrastination that is the problem. However...

Beyond merely an aggravation and inconvenience, is procrastination perhaps a warning sign? The body has many mechanisms to protect us from perceived danger and procrastination may be one of them.

We naturally push ahead doing things when we don't see the need to act on right away. To **use procrastination wisely**, we should stop, pause for a beat, and ask ourselves:

"Wait a minute - does this action need more thinking through?"

If I procrastinate and put this off, is there a good reason why? Is this discomfort with this task a warning sign that I should really be paying some attention to?

Checking for alignment with values and with commitment to the activity, to a person, or to the task....is doing this activity a good idea?

Lack of alignment with what you want and should be doing can manifest as discomfort; here procrastination is a good thing, a warning sign which should *not* to be ignored, and passed over as routine 'bad' behavior.

Here's What Happens in the Brain during Procrastination

First, we visually see something - a big project - that we don't want to do.

Physically seeing it activates the insular cortex, a brain region associated with pain,   which then causes a physical neural discomfort, which is short-term and will go away soon enough, but still gives an initial ick feeling of "*I don't want to do this*" accompanied by a real discomfort sensation.

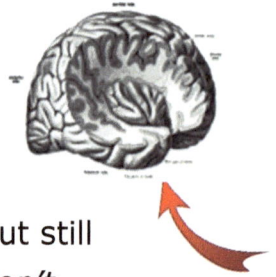

The brain seeks to shut down the pain (who wants to feel discomfort?) so looks to shift attention to something else, to move off of the pain (get a yummy snack!

Take a break! Procrastinate this activity!)

So procrastination leads to a short but immediate feeling of pleasure – it sure feels good to take a break!

But when that temporary pleasant feeling fades and it's time to go back and face the original task that was procrastinated...

...the discomfort is even greater on the return than it was initially, for having put it off. The little discomfort suddenly becomes a bigger discomfort due to procrastinating it!

Reasons for Procrastination

There are several reasons why we tend to procrastinate:

PERFECTIONISM – oh, those mile **high standards**! So high, in fact, that the project can never really get done because it will never be completely perfect. So it gets put off as an **endless job that will never be right,** right against our impossible standards. Let's procrastinate away THAT project, which will take too much

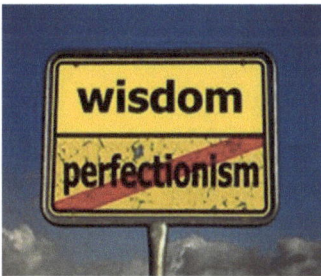

time to complete properly, at which point we've moved on and have lost interest.

REBEL AGAINST BEING FORCED

(self-forced or forced by outside pressures) to undertake obligatory actions - procrastination can be a **small act of rebellion** against doing something we would rather not be **forced to do** *"I'm not going to do this right now"*

NOT ORGANIZED yet to begin - messy

desk, clutter, project not organized – **lack of preparedness causes delays.** And the thought of the pre-preparation work that's needed to start just expands the size of the task; it's easy to procrastinate when the scope of what's involved gets even bigger...

FRUSTRATION compounded

by excessive procrastination causes even more procrastination

STRUCTURED PROCRASTINATION: the false sense of making progress, which is really just **busy work not real work**. We easily fool ourselves into thinking were making progress when it's not really happening. That busy work surely looks and even feels good, but where's the true forward movement of results?

Getting on Top of Procrastination

One theory is that all it takes to overcome procrastination is strong **willpower** – with self-discipline, self-control – we can **power our way to focus** on the goal and stay there.

The problem with willpower is that we **only have a finite amount** of it every day, usually greatest in the morning, which **becomes depleted** over the course of the day. This theory says the best course of action is to power up the big projects early in the morning when willpower and focus are at peak levels.

However to power through a project on willpower alone **requires a lot of neural energy**; the brain being an energy hog, uses up 20% of the body's energy supply. Pulling much of the brain's available energy for sustained focus is **hard to maintain**.

Plus that process is **easily derailed by negative self-talk** *("I'm not going to do a good enough job"; "My efforts aren't not going to meet with so-and-so's approval",* etc.) and so we procrastinate, *"I don't feel like doing this job right now; I'll do it later."*

How to Get Motivated

Tackle the big tasks first – find the motivation behind the tasks by connecting emotionally with the task itself, by thinking about the impact of the outcome.

- Visually what will you see when the task is completed?

- What tangible outcome will happen as a result of doing the task?

- Who is affected by the completed result what will the impact be on the people involved?

Also helpful is being reminded of the original kernel of inspiration that got the task started in the first place, such as having a visual cue of the desired outcome.

Using any of these techniques gives good inspiration to start the task versus procrastinate doing it.

Audacity can be inspiring!

Distractions Can Take Us Off Course

It's just too easy to lose focus and get derailed if distractions aren't contained –

Tune out, turn off, turn away entirely if necessary for a **designated period of time** to wholly focus on the task:

Ignore your email

Silence your phone

Turn off all other electronics

- **Get in the zone**, let distractions flow by, relax into the flow of the work
- **Focus on living in the present moment**; stop self-judgment from creeping in – thoughts like *"Am I close to the end yet?"* are not in flow!
- If it's quick (takes only 2 mins), do the distracting activity now, if it takes more than 2 mins, put it on the To Do List – **be strict with the 2-min rule!**

Create Urgency

Plan **small step deadlines inside of the big project** deadline, then remind yourself about each time deadline repeatedly and frequently.

Procrastination is a <u>Keystone</u>* BAD HABIT

Habits are in place to save brain energy – we don't have to do any serious thinking with the automatic behavior that habits provide.

Habits are powerful because they create neurological cravings; the brain craves the pleasurable feeling, the payoff reward, which habits deliver.

*Keystone habits influence other important areas in life.

Once procrastination is recognize as a keystone bad habit, chronic procrastination can be worked on and changed.

How habits work:

→ Starts with a trigger – the cue that sets off the habit, which can be:

Location, visual (seeing something triggers a habit)

Time (we follow habits at

certain times of the day)

Feeling (bored? – habits are often cued by feelings)

Reaction (when I do this, I then do that, in lock step)

→ With automatic habits we are **often unaware** of when the habit begins; we frequently have no idea of the habit's trigger.

To figure out what gets the procrastination habit started, you need to be present minded, notice the moment an avoidance trap starts – quick! What was the immediately preceding cue? - then **shift the reaction to the specific trigger.**

→ After the trigger cues the habit, a set routine takes place. The ensuing procrastination routine behavior can only be successfully re-wired with a PLAN: devise new routines (i.e. special alarm ringtone to start the task instead of putting it off; i.e. take a few deep breaths then start; i.e. 5-min stretch activity then start) and new specific tasks each day.

Focusing on the <u>process</u> (time you will start and stop + new routine to follow), **NOT focusing on the product** (stop focusing on the outcome that will result) will lead to successfully not procrastinating.

> Every habit has a reward, an immediate pleasure feeling.
>   - Recognize the payoff for procrastinating (that short term pleasure described above) and **reframe it** with the truth that procrastination is really just a short term pleasure, soon replaced by greater pain.
>
>   - **Replace the old payoff with a new reward** (tangible or intangible) that is in the new routine you create.

- ○ **Delay the new reward until you finish** the task.

(Yes, *self-training* can be like dog training!)

➢ Supporting every habit is an underlying belief; change this to change the habit.

Belief in the new plan - that it will work and that it is better than the old habit – is a critical piece for success.

This is most easily done with the **support of a friend or of a group**/community. Tell people you know what you're doing, to support your efforts to change the habit.

Deal with Procrastination

Here are 6 good ways to deal with procrastination -

1. Become a TIME TRAVELER -

Think ahead to the future and imagine your life when in that future:

... You have **completed the task** and are **receiving wonderful accolades** for the good job, which is **much appreciated by those impacted** by the work

OR, is it an alternative future where:

... You procrastinated **too long** and now you're so **regretful** for doing so; more than uncomfortable, you are now **facing serious consequences** for your lapse

Imagining either future, good or bad, is motivating to stop procrastinating.

2. Write a **TO DO LIST** –

...the night before, which gives the **brain time to work** on the best way to achieve success **while you're sleeping**

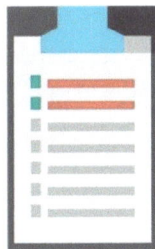

3. **CHUNK DOWN** the task –

...into **small doable steps** that can be completed in a smaller time frame and lead to a satisfying feeling of completion. *Small success gratification is more satisfying than the feeling of making progress* towards completing the overall big goal.

4. Pomodoro: commit to focusing on the task in **20-MIN TIME PERIODS** –

Schedule in these short working time periods on your calendar, take a **break after 20-min** of sustained focus,

plan small rewards when each period is over, and plan **a big reward for when the full task/project is fully completed**.

5. BELIEVE IN THE PLAN –
Really trust that it will work, or it won't have a fighting chance of success! **Your mind controls your own success.**

6. HAVE A BACKUP -
Every good plan has a planned backup, for when **things go awry, which they inevitably will do.** Slipups are OK, as long as you know what to do when they happen. Don't be caught short without a backup action plan to follow, **or the old habit will be the default action** in the void of an alternative.

PLAN B

The SmartyPants Secret on PROCRASTINATION

PROCRASTINATING is a <u>keystone habit</u>, influencing other important areas of life; so procrastinating little things can result in accumulative damage down the road.

You have a choice, to become your own master, instead of letting your habits master you.

BOOK BUYER BONUS

As a thank you to buyers, there is an additional free resource available only to book buyers. Did you get yours? If you missed it, go to www.SmartyPantsSecrets.com/bookbonus .

It has additional valuable content and is free to book buyers, so don't miss out on getting yours!

BOOK RESOURCE

Every SmartyPants Secrets book has a companion resource on the topic that may be of interest. The resource for this Procrastination Book is a **100% natural organic _Herbal Blend Procrastination Cease Aid_, to support ceasing to procrastinate.**

This **_Herbal Blend Procrastination Cease Aid_** not only works to support ceasing to procrastinate, it also tastes great. Know anyone else experiencing a similar problem procrastinating that they want support with?

For ordering and other information on this and other SmartyPants Secrets support products, visit the website at www.SmartyPantsSecrets.com/resources

ABOUT ME

I am DR Martin, PhD* (*Personal human Development expertise) – Dolley Rapoport Martin. I took Dolley as my first name* in honor of the great First Lady Dolley Madison, whom I admire for her heroic actions in the White House during very turbulent times.

I took Rapoport as a middle name* in honor of Ingeborg Rapoport, who at age 103, is the oldest person to be awarded a Doctorate; finally getting the recognition due her from 77 years prior in Nazi Germany, unfairly denied her due to her Jewish roots. There is so much injustice in the world; it is an honor to recognize her achievement by taking her name. [*The selecting of one's name is an important exercise, since names are so personal and tied to identity. Yet most of us go through life with a name not of our choosing. Check out the SmartyPants Secret book NAMES.]

I have studied every communication subject for more than a decade, acquiring a large body of knowledge. I, perhaps like you, am a voracious reader and learner. My other strength is that I retain much of what I learn, so I can then compile the knowledge on a variety of subjects into a concise format, making the books that I author a shortcut on the best knowledge available. This saves you from going through all the data looking for the kernel that makes the greatest difference in success, the SmartyPants secret on a given topic.

I also have a mind that is ever curious about so many topics. I have earned multiple expert designations (education certified English teacher, Real Estate Broker, Stock Broker series 7, series 6, series, Certified Financial Manager, Insurance producer certified, Coach University) and held high level positions in business – large corporate entities, privately held companies, non-profit organizations, and startups – and have volunteered extensively, holding executive positions at the local, district and national levels. So I've been around the block more than once, on more than one topic.

Due to my research and experience, I have logged the perquisite time to carry the title of expert, giving myself an honorary PhD in the expertise area of communication, Personal human Development. I am passionate about sharing the knowledge that I have gained with you, in bite-size pieces.

And when a certain topic is not in my field of expertise, I find an expert with deep expertise in the field who has the knowledge that I seek. I then ask numerous in-depth questions of the expert to get to the gist, learn the SmartyPants Secret, then pass the knowledge on in a book on the subject.

For other titles and additional resources, visit www.SmartyPantsSecrets.com

Watch for content clips and helpful technique tips on a variety of topics coming soon at www.youtube.com/c/smartypantssecrets

Contact: Info@SmartyPantsSecrets.com

www.ingramcontent.com/pod-product-compliance
Lightning Source LLC
Chambersburg PA
CBHW041226270326
41934CB00001B/24